SEE YOU IN THE DARK

SEE YOU IN THE DARK

LYNNE SHARON SCHWARTZ

Poems

CURBSTONE BOOKS

NORTHWESTERN UNIVERSITY PRESS

EVANSTON, ILLINOIS

Curbstone Books
Northwestern University Press
www.nupress.northwestern.edu

Printed in the United States of America

10 9 8 7 6 5 4 3 2 1

Library of Congress Cataloging-in-Publication Data
Schwartz, Lynne Sharon.
    See you in the dark : poems / Lynne Sharon Schwartz.
      p. cm.
    Poems, some previously published.
    Includes bibliographical references.
    ISBN 978-0-8101-2799-9 (pbk. : alk. paper)
    I. Title.
  PS3569.C567S44 2011
  811.54—dc22

                        2011026626

CONTENTS

II

III

ACKNOWLEDGMENTS

The following poems and short prose pieces appeared first in these publications: "Coda" in *Agni;* "Flu" in *Ascent;* "Sleeping Dancers" in *Denver Quarterly;* "Hurricanes" in the *Iowa Review;* "The Key" in *Poet Lore;* "Projections," "First Fig at Fifty," and "Sarah and Jack Dancing in 1959" in *Poetry East;* "Pink Tree," "TraumaMan," "Christmas Cactus," "The Impossible Dream," "Untranslatable," "Butterfly in the Lecture Hall," and "How to Approach a New Idea" in *Prairie Schooner;* "The Afterlife" in *River Styx;* "Woman . . . According to the Movies" in *Salamander;* "Not Quite Gone" in the *Seattle Review;* and "Near November" in the anthology *110 Stories* (NYU Press, 2002).

SEE YOU IN THE DARK

GREETING

Go, little book, where I cannot.
Greet the strangers as they dream,
Turning pages, seeking what?
Speculation, omen, gleam,
Everything twixt be and seem.

May the lines please, if just a day,
Nor roughly bruise the inner ear.
Before they scatter, let them say
Do you read me? Are you there?
What are these words but ink and air?

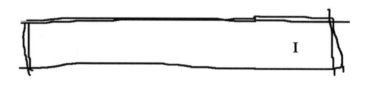

I

PINK TREE

That tree resplendent in her sudden pink
flowering, what does she think
of the outrageous brevity of her glory?
Bare all year, now overnight grown gorgeous
as a girl in a trembling hoop skirt
poised to whirl across the ballroom floor,
she's at the mercy of the wind astride the river.
Six days, maybe eight, or ten at best,
before it strips her back to bone.

Is she as flared with joy as she appears,
basking in the sunstruck scrutiny
of her dazzled fans below,
greeting them regally: see me,
behold my finery?

                    Or could she be
already brooding on the week ahead
when she'll be all in tatters, and the bitter
season soon to come, like seasons past,
long and arduous and melancholic.
She knows the chill she'll feel at the wind's sweep,
the way she'll start and shake,
helpless and raging at its ravages,
seething yet again at the injustice.
Was it worth the tedious wait and work
for six meager days of brilliant pink?

Meanwhile in a premonitory breeze
scatters of blown petals rip loose
to flutter down, unwilling, where young girls
pluck them from the grass to deck their hair.

Apricots, melons—she was no stranger
to the pleasures of the fleshy fruits,
yet never knew till late the intricate
squishiness of the delicious
fig, the pink, seedy, soft, fleshy,
oh so sweet and messy—
eating them you can't be neat—fig,
suspicious fruit, the purple outside dull, deceptive,
shading into black, the other kind, lime green,
more cunning, faintly sickly, still perversely
tempting, both
the same inside ripe joy of absolute
fruition, their sweetness on the tongue a vast
relief, so easy, yielding.
How could she have lived so long
not knowing? Now
she sucks them slowly, wallowing
in figs, figs, and more figs. Yes,
it's good to wait, to be surprised
by treasures. Yes,
she's glad
she came to figs so late.

THE IMPOSSIBLE DREAM

In my young dreams I drove
runaway cars down flights of steps,
into the hurling tide, or off steep cliffs.
I woke near death, gasping with relief.

Now I dream the same but never wake.
The hurtling car negotiates the steps,
the cliff, the sea. I pump the brake,
grip the wheel, firm my mind, survive,

and drive. Perhaps it's time that's made me brave
in dreams at least. But I suspect
I've merely lost my dread

and halfway long to throw myself away.
Once an ancient woman said to me,
You think you die so easy? Wait and see.

Filthy refs, my father from the car window
in stalled traffic shouted every Saturday
at the Jews who embarrassed him, spilling
into the streets, their long Polish coats,
the wispy hair, the fur hats, the women offensively
drab, trailing the waxy-faced children,
my mother in the front seat shushing him,
but he not letting up: Filthy refs,
you think you own the streets? My mother moaned,
scolded, For Chrissake, you were one yourself,
how can you talk that way? and he:
I never looked like that, while I, stiff,
silently egging them on from the back seat,
understanding them all too well, wishing
one or the other would finally win,
rage or compassion, which, I didn't care—
anything but this endless joined battle—
and most of all, wanting, waiting—
When, oh when can I get out of here?

At the end of the street of tidy row houses
DeSotos in the driveways, suddenly
that declivity, dirt hill, shrunken valley,
shambly patch with three wooden houses,
shacks, really, chickens poking at pebbles.
We took that shortcut down to school,
in winter sledded down that hill. The people
were foreign, ill clothed, stocky, speaking
nothing we could understand. Some days
the fat old lady eyed us from her doorway—
hands on aproned hips, thin hair, no teeth.
We fled, we said she had the evil eye.

When she trudged up the street with her net bag
we'd scatter and hide, screeching, Witch, witch.
Carol the Witch, we called her. She shuffled on,
her gray head bent, those wisps of hair forlorn,
maybe she didn't know the word. I hope
she didn't. This was Brooklyn,
after the war, cruel ignorant children.
Forgive us, Carol. I don't know your real name.

The child covers her face
to be invisible.
I—the obverse—when you refused
to see me, disappeared.

How obediently I succumbed,
shrank, numbed,
only my visions stayed,
of bloody violence.

Erased by oversight, by grace
awakened, now I write
pointy words, every prick of the pen
a gash in your flesh.

FLU

Rampant, it strikes the strongest soon or late,
like love, like death.
Yet it has its virtues too, the flu—
not the flu of chills and fever and tormented breath
but the mild kind, the kindly,
like a languid childhood illness
of bed and solitude, no school,
just books and soup
and colored pictures drifting through the mind.

The muscles melt to pudding and a heavy
lassitude spreads its sweet stillness,
like love, like death.
Give in: this flu will pass. It does not last.

Good for nothing as we are—
and this nothing feels incomparably good,
like love, if not like death—
we dream our past all day,
like drowning, so they say.

And in the light of—no, the shadow of—the flu
(the flu's light is a tender shade of blue)
our past looks like a wasted patch
of tattered ground and scattered energies,
a confusion we pursued
with an alien exertion quite beyond us as we lie,
undone by flu, its flickering blue,
a confusion we suspect invited in this flu,
insinuating stealthily like love,
like death.

Then one day comes a quickening
of forces in the melted, fallow muscles
and the murmuring blood that whispers on a breath,
Rest now, because, alas,
like love, if not like death,
this flu will not last.

TRAIL

The homeless man on drugs is walking, no,
loping, or, better still, bopping,
a sideways, almost hopping motion from foot
to foot, down our street, tearing, as he
goes, strips of white bread from the sandwich
in his hand, dropping them on the sidewalk,
not alms for the birds, like the early morning
pigeon lady, rather, oversized bites.
Showing his contempt, maybe—
our smug, swept street—yet maybe not,
maybe leaving a trail, as he tracks
his demon into the wooded park beyond,
into the forest, into the hut in its dark
heart, hoping for someone to follow after,
to the rescue, bringing back the bread.

Little Greek fish with no name,
you came in a mound on a platter,
fried, succulent, praised by the waiter
in that café on the beach, Aegean water
lapping under the moon. We tried
all the names we knew of small fish—
sardines, anchovies, smelts, herring, minnows—
but he kept shaking his head—
no English name.
In Greek? He shrugged: We call them little fish.

Little fish, size of minnows but not minnows,
fish as fine as you deserve a name.
When I want to revive that summer night,
the soft air on our skin, the skimming surf,
the stars, the shiny fish
we ate with our fingers, a savory, garlicky fishy
flavor, I want a word. Without a word
memory's a cloud I can't slide
my hand around.
Little fish, how did you glide
so nimbly past the translators?

PICKLES

Lolling in their briny pool
souring slowly by degree
in chest-high barrels, one two three,
for pickles we would rush and cry
pickles daily after school

aproned pickle man would pluck
pickles out with metal tongs
sell them to us for a song
two or three cents, big ones five
eat them slowly, lick and suck

pickles salty wet and tart
made our tongues recoil and smart
made our eyes heat up and tear
oh where are the pickles of yesteryear?

READING THE HAIR

1

Hieroglyphics on the bathtub tiles
send a slender message:
I curl, says the hair,
I snap and crackle, I shall not
stay put. However hard you try
with brush and iron, blower, spray or dye,
you shall never be
one of the tamed and smooth of tress.
Your head is stuck with me,
unruly.

2

In junior high we girls would yank one
from our muddled heads to see
how many knots could be tied in a single hair
and with each knot called out the name of a boy.
When the hair broke,
that was our destined boy. But the hair lied.

3

My mother's kinky hair, born brown,
in midlife reinvented in persimmon red,
then briefly blond—a failed experiment—
returned to red where it remained
till she lay dead,
hair far too merry for a face worn out by dread.

4

Is the hair an outward sign
of weather in the head? A bad hair day
would mean a day of flaccid, messy mind.

No, for then the bald would be
forever empty headed, harebrained. That's not so:
think of the clever baldies we all know.
The hair's text can't be trusted. Look at me,
my stubborn mop suggests a mind
bristly and wild, defiant. Maybe once,
but now my hair stays lively
while my head inside
goes slack and mild.

SAINT ALEXIUS'S MOTHER

Seventeen years we sheltered the holy man.
We took him in when he came begging
a place to sleep. Euphemianus, my husband,
offered a decent bed but the man would have
only the nook below the cellar stairs,
ate nothing but gruel, so thin he was, all bone,
so holy, always praying, barely sleeping,
rarely speaking, not even saying his name,
yet thanking us daily for the food and shelter.
This morning the servant bringing him his bowl
found him crumpled on the floor, his eyes
stark and staring, skin stiff and cold.

Preparing the body for the laying out,
we found in the folds of his robe writings
that told of his holy life, signed Alexius,
Alexius, the name of our beloved son
who fled to escape the marriage we'd arranged—
the daughter of a fine Roman family.
Alexius, always stubborn, refused the match.
He must give his life to God, he said,
and ran away. This corpse, our vanished son.
We never recognized the boy we raised,
so much had holy hunger altered him.
Seventeen years, our son, the saintly man,

wasting in the hole below the stairs.
Why did he choose our door and not another?
Was it a yearning to be close by, or was it
vicious pleasure taken in deception?
Does love of God blind saints to other loves,
to the starved heart of a mother without her son?

Or was he waiting to be recognized?
What kind of mother doesn't know her son?
I cursed myself
when I learned his name and hugged his holy bones.
I curse Alexius for his cruelty.
Tell me, my son, what holiness was this?

The mail continues, merciless. A questionnaire:
Please help us rate the quality of care
at our facility. First, were you satisfied
with the services our staff
endeavored to provide?
Were you treated courteously,
your needs addressed efficiently?
Would you say that you received the very best
of medical attention? No or yes?
Was there sufficient consultation
regarding your post-discharge situation?
In short, fill in: poor, good, or excellent.

Since the questionnaire's recipient
was in no state to rate, her son replied.
I never was discharged at all, he wrote.
It's not a question of dissatisfied.
Simply—I'm surprised you don't
recall—I died.

SLEEPING WITH HIM

By day so democratic and discreet,
in sleep despotic,
all crushing tentacle,
the weight of arm and leg
dragging me down his dreams
on twisted paths of sheets.

Blessed nights,
beguiled by the hot maze of him.
I keep vigil, hoarding every instant
of the skin on skin.

Light streaks in, we leap
apart, we veer to polar distances,
waving—till later, darling,
see you in the dark.

BUTTERFLY IN THE LECTURE HALL

For Sinan Antoon

The lecturer was grave,
speaking of exile, poets uprooted,
refusing to brood in silence, bravely singing
of freedom, when the butterfly appeared
flitting above his head, swooping, distracting

the audience by its sweeping
designs, swirls etched on air
as the speaker, rapt, pursued
the trail of injustice, forced flight, unaware
of this other, extravagant flight,

which seemed a ploy
to mock his somber theme, a frivolous
airborne blossom teasing his PowerPoints
with "lighten up." But when it lingered past
the instant of surprise, I knew

the butterfly was sent to illustrate
the dartings of the speaker's thought,
the flighty pattern of a fertile mind,
the freedom of its arabesques, the force
of thought assuming visible wings:
a butterfly.

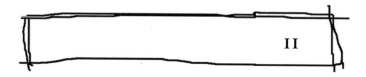

II

HOW TO APPROACH A NEW IDEA

By stealth,
on tiptoe
holding your breath
not to scare
or waken too abruptly
rousing fear
of being roughly
mauled or scarred,
crudely taken,
and ensnared.

Use discretion
when it quivers,
soothe its trembling
with assurance
of respect and every due
consideration
for its subtlety
and guarded
possibilities,
its secret convolutions

its future evolutions.
Once you cup it
in your palm
keep it warm,
never rushing
lightly touching.
If you prod or hasten
it will crouch and curl.
Let it unfurl in its time,
exposing each striation.

If it trusts you
it will yield
intimate initiation—
what unparalleled elation.

They shambled in, a flock of sweet
disheveled sheep,
herded to the water lilies.
"See this picture?" said the teacher.
"It was painted by a man who lived
long ago, his name was Mr. Monet.
What do you think that Mr. Monet was thinking
when he saw those pretty lily pads?"

Ah, Mr. Monet, what were you thinking?
Why is the world so overcast with red?
My eyes, poor eyes, those wretched cataracts.
Please let the light stay light for five more minutes.

Tell them, Ms. Teacher, how Mr. Renoir's fingers
were so deformed and stiff from the arthritis,
he had to strap the brushes to his hands.
Mr. Michelangelo developed a chronic backache
from that infernal ceiling, and Mr. Matisse
spent his last years sitting in his bed,
playing with his scissors and his paste.
Mr. Van Gogh suffered in his mind,
his ear a holy wound.

Tell them that art is hard.
It takes the life right out of you,
and gives it back in paint, in pain.
It's hard, *mes enfants,* art is hard.

PROJECTIONS

*(Jenny Holzer projects poetry on the façade of the New York Public
Library from dusk to midnight, October 6 to 9, 2005.)*

The words, made of light,
rise out of darkness
to slither up the library steps,
block letters climbing: the steps,
the columns, up into the arches,
broken by the walls of the arches,
losing some letters in their recesses,
then climbing higher to reassemble,
gather the lost letters,
slide up the frieze,
ascend to the pediment
and upward, into the night sky,
the words invisible now,
filling the air above Fifth Avenue.

Over and over, the words
rise out of nothingness,
sliding up from darkness to the steps,
climbing the columns,
arches, frieze, pediment,
sky, over and over,
and the air above the library filled with books
is filled with words, escaped
like cooped-up children freed.
The air is dense with words.
The world is made words again as,
in the beginning, the Logos,
starting with the word made light,
and climbing.

ARS POETICA, OR SOUP

Dedicated to the puffy man
at the party given to honor the writers,
who said, upon discovering I had children,
Oh, so, you're just a housewife who writes.
Thirty years ago, that was. Maybe today
he'd know better.

To be a housewife who writes,
start with soup.
Choose the proper pot, the right shape
to embrace your soup. Heavy or light,
tall or squat, the pot
will determine how the soup develops.
A pot with a lid—soup needs privacy to grow.

Begin with a meaty bone, for structure,
then turn your thoughts to water.
Water is the idiom of the soup,
whether thick or a clear broth. Water:
the music the ingredients will dance to,
the medium they'll swim in, tasteless to start,
but soon absorbing the flavor of carrots,
parsnips, celery, leeks, turnips, kale,
or mushrooms, to be added sequentially—
first the hard, later the soft,
some chopped up fine, some left in chunks. Consider
the feeling you wish to achieve upon the tongue.

Stir the mixture with a wooden spoon.
Watch it coalesce. You may require
some unanticipated ingredient.
Hunt that ingredient out,

no matter how far you must travel.
Watch your soup at all times.
Do not desert it for other endeavors. Wait
for the dazzling moment when it resembles soup,
deserves the esteemed name, soup.

Near the end, add spices, not mere salt,
but fearlessly the more exotic, curry,
coriander, cardamom, or tarragon,
to awaken your soup, like a god's breath
infused in clay. Now the soup will want to chart

its own nature and destiny. Now the power relations
between you and your soup become delicate,
demanding negotiation, give and take.
Yield, when you can, to the wisdom of the soup.

As it approaches its consummation
remove the stripped bone, the original armature,
an awkward procedure but necessary,
in the service of the soup.

While it cools,
straighten up the house to make it ready.
Sweep, dust, scrub, but not too carefully.
Soup will not thrive in a sterile atmosphere.

Summon the guests to the table and serve your soup.

The healthy plant outgrows its pot
the way a healthy child outgrows its clothes.
Don't let it suffer constriction. Spread the Sports
or Business section of the *New York Times*
on the dining room table. Find a clay pot
big enough for fresh growth. In the bottom
place pebbles and shards from a broken pot for drainage.
Add handfuls of moist black potting soil,
digging your hands deep in the bag, rooting
so the soil gets under your fingernails.
Using a small spade or butter knife,
ease the plant out of its old pot with extreme
care so as not to disturb its wiry roots.

The plant is naked, suspended from your hand
like a newborn, roots and clinging soil
exposed. Treat it gently. Settle it
into the center of the new pot, adding soil
on the sides for support—who isn't shaky,
moving into a new home?
Pack more soil around the plant,
tapping it down till you almost reach the rim.
Flounce the leaves as you would a skirt. Then water.
Place the pot back on the shelf in the sunlight.
Gather the Sports section around the spilled soil
and discard. Watch your plant flourish.
You have done a good and necessary deed.

In ancient times, to be a proper Druid,
the rigorous initiation rite
required the applicant to lie all night
in a narrow coffin, drenched in fluid—

an inch or two of water, more or less—
and while he soaks from toe to nose
he must with all due haste compose
a poem of distinction and finesse,

on a topic preassigned,
plus—as if that task alone were not sufficient—
he must, although his talent be deficient
and however much he might be disinclined,

devise a fitting music, stately measures,
then prepare for a rendition—
if he hasn't yet expired from attrition—
for the senior Druids' morning listening pleasures.

You poets who bemoan your lack of standing,
and covet glory and high reputations,
give thanks you're spared the Druids' tribulations:
to be ignored is tough, but less demanding.

MAN WITH UNSPOKEN WORDS

As much as he talked—
and he talked so much,
often in a haste approaching frenzy—
he never said, or so it seemed, the words
he needed most to say, most needed us

to hear, the words that would make plain
the spate of other, needless words.
He would grow so excited by the pressure
of those straining words that craved
release, the air around him trembled

with their clatter. And all the while we tried
to show ourselves prepared to hear
what his flushed face and uneasy eyes
hinted could barely be suppressed an instant
longer. Still, by evening's end,

the end of every evening in his urgent
presence, that fevered cordiality,
the words remained unspoken, receding
from the verge,
although the sway and tremble of the air

was in no way diminished, as though the words
rocked on its currents, and only our clumsy deafness
caused, as we said good night, his gloom
and fret at yet another visit failed.
We never heard the words. Yet afterwards,

we'd wonder, Could it be he said them?
Could we, in our earnest readiness
to hear, have missed them?

TRAUMAMAN

I heard about him on the radio.
What a doll!
I wish I had one for my very own
to keep in thrall.
They say he's just a torso, not all there,
but I don't care.

When he's opened up he's quite complete
with skin and blood and bone
all marvelously neat,
every organ where it should be but
not the coils of gut.
He's several thousand bucks yet that's a steal

for med schools where they need to operate—
carve, extract, reorganize, and sew—
on someone less than real.
A sorry fate,
which no one else would bear without a moan
except this willing drone.

Praise TraumaMan: thus surgeons learn to heal.
Why can't we all have one to see us through
those moments when we long to wield the knife
but hesitate to scar a human life?
You can cut him time and time again
and patient TraumaMan will feel no pain—

at least he won't complain.

MAN . . . ACCORDING TO THE MOVIES

Of a thousand faces, on the moon,

who fell to Earth in the white suit,

with the golden arm,

who knew too much—with two brains—

of the West, from Laramie, from the Alamo,

who shot Liberty Valance in the saddle,

who would be king

of flowers, of iron, of marble,

who came to dinner

in the gray flannel suit

with one red shoe, in love

with the golden gun, with cat dancing,

who loved women for all seasons

Escaped

in the iron mask

alone

without a star

In red, in the dunes

of the prehistoric planet

next door,

under the influence

of affairs, of Paris, of the year,

without love, rebels,

in love,

on the verge of a nervous breakdown,

is a woman.

TWO FROM CATULLUS

LVIII

Caeli, Lesbia nostra, Lesbia illa,
illa Lesbia, quam Catullus unam
plus quam se atque suos amavit omnes,
nunc in quadriviis et angiportis
glubit magnanimi Remi nepotes.

Oh Caelius, our Lesbia, that Lesbia,
the very Lesbia Catullus used to love
more than himself and all he owned on earth,
these days hangs out in Rome's dark alleyways
jerking off the sons of the noble city.

LXXXV

Odi et amo, quare id faciam, fortasse requiris?
nescio, sed fieri sentio et excrucior.

I hate and love—you ask how this can be?
Who knows? And yet the feeling tears at me.

When as a college student I first encountered Verlaine's most famous poem, I was delighted and enchanted. As with long familiarity of so many kinds, enchantment can lead irresistibly to parody. What follows are the original and successively diminished English versions.

Il pleure dans mon coeur

Il pleut doucement sur la ville.
(Arthur Rimbaud)

Il pleure dans mon coeur
Comme il pleut dans la ville;
Quelle est cette langueur
Qui pénètre mon coeur?

O bruit doux de la pluie
Par terre et sur les toits!
Pour un coeur qui s'ennuie
O le chant de la pluie!

Il pleure sans raison
Dans ce coeur qui s'écoeure.
Quoi! nulle trahison?...
Ce deuil sans raison.

C'est bien la pire peine
De ne savoir pourquoi
Sans amour et sans haine
Mon coeur a tant de peine!

My heart weeps with rain
As it pours all through town
And the languorous pain
has quite soaked my brain.

Oh the sweet lulling sound
Makes my heart grow so slack
As the roofs and the ground
Sing the song of the drowned.

My tears defy all reason
In this sickened heart.
If I've suffered no treason
Why so blue out of season?

This is the worst of fates,
To be without a clue:
I feel no love or hate,
Yet my heart precipitates.

My heart's drenched with weeping
As rains drench downtown.
A languor comes creeping.
Into my heart it's seeping.

The soft strains are a lull
On sidewalk and roof.
For a heart grown so dull,
How sweet sounds the lull.

It weeps for no reason
my poor stricken heart.
No betrayals, no treason,
Simply grief past all reason.

And the worst thing to bear
Is not knowing why,
Lacking love, hate, or care
I persist in despair.

Outside, rain.
Inside, grief.
Why such pain?
What's my beef?

Patter sweet,
on roofs and street:
to heart so sore
that song's a treat.

Sick, in thrall
to senseless tears.
No cause at all
For such a pall.

My heart won't dry
and worst of all,
I can't say why
I love to cry.

This here's the house
where Frank and Jesse lived, till the raid
last month. We stood in the snow
right here on the Grand Concourse
and watched them carried off in cuffs.
No better neighbors ever lived, those James boys,
always helping out with cash for rent,
food at the local bodega, bikes for the kids.
They robbed the rich to give the poor,
Frank said, and seeing as we're the poor,
it's ours to take
what should be ours by right.

Now they rot on Rikers while the rich
rest easy, them who rob on paper. Rumors say
they got some famous cousins, brothers too,
the one a Harvard prof, the other off
in England, writing books. If blood
was really thicker, like they say, than water,
those other James boys would put in a word,
get Frank and Jesse off the hook.
Their story'd make a book all right.
But highfalutin types like those, I bet
they never even seen the Bronx
nor know the fix their kin is in or care.

THE BOY OBSESSED

Whatever became of the boy—Barry, Terry?
no, Tony—who at fifteen was obsessed
with death, said he stayed up half the night
pondering the mystery, staring
at the furniture that would outlast him.
He carried on incessantly, we thought
he'd go crazy, almost hoped he would,
for the sheer drama. At parties
he'd wave his arms and shout:
Don't you get it, all of this, all of us,
will disappear, as if we never were?
We shall be no more! We laughed,
he had a witty way about him, Tony, debonair,
he relished his obsession. On he'd rant,
the couples on the couch would glance up,
then resume their necking, the dancers
pressed more tightly into each other's torsos,
the boys' hands edging towards a breast,
others would shrug, grab a soda from the fridge,
open a bag of chips, change the record and—
Death, death! he'd shout again. How can we endure
each day, knowing the inevitable?
His girlfriend murmured, Enough now, Tony,
give it a rest.
Death never rests, he'd say, laying his head in her lap.

A clever boy, he wouldn't waste his life.
He must have subsided into the common way,
making the most of his looks, brains, charm,
and if he ever thought of his obsession,

dismissed it as boyish self-indulgence, till
fifty years on, the suspicion grows
that he had it right, way back. Winter nights
he lays his head on his sleeping wife's breast
and whispers his old words . . . No more . . .
as if we never were.

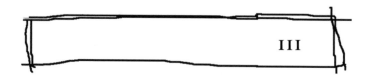

III

Canny as pickpockets
they spot each other instantly.
No need for secret grips or amulets,
only the mute passwords, clever lips,
a slant of eyelids, millimeter
signal of the head, the body's quick
stillness, poised like a cat found
where it shouldn't be, alert, unfazed.
Just so, it's all arranged.
They make their moves in stealth,

leaving no trace.
They love in haste,
novelty their pique and their delight.
In multiplicity
they re-create—as many selves as loves.

Outlaws, they walk among us in plain sight,
guiltless—they know no rule.
They have no wish to hurt
or to desert. Simply, they crave
the game. Love is their craft and guild,
betrayal the dues they pay.
If deft deception is a trade,
are the faithless born to it or made?

EMOTION

I keep telling you baby don't give it away
all at once like you like to do,
give it in little sips, just enough
to keep them coming back thirsty
Nobody's supply is endless and
there is no goddamn law says
you got to give your all all the time

But you never did listen to common sense
so why am I wasting my breath
I guess you'll just keep on
spilling over like a fucking river
then running dry till the next rainfall
though you know a man don't like
no dried-up woman

You were the boy with the crew cut sitting on my left in the Phoenix Theater on Twelfth Street, a Sunday matinee in September. I was the girl dressed all in black, alone. Do you remember me? Please let me know. I stayed in my seat during the intermission to work on the *Times* crossword puzzle. The theme was existentialism. I wrote Simone de Beauvoir, across, and you leaned over and with your pencil wrote *The Mandarins,* down. The play was Shaw's *Saint Joan,* starring Siobhan McKenna, who is gone now, as is the Phoenix Theater. If you remember all this please be in touch. I would like to talk to you again the way we did when we went for coffee after the play, then rode back to Brooklyn on the subway. I got off at Utica Avenue and you continued on. The next night you called. Do you have any recollection of this? I had a date with a tall blond boy who had tickets to the Budapest String Quartet but I broke it. We talked on the phone till late, that night and many other nights. We got married and raised two children. You must remember that. I would love to talk to you again, to ask you, after so many years, how it has been for you, what you think about your life spent with me, and in particular what possessed you to write on my puzzle so boldly and impressively, *The Mandarins,* because I think that was why I married you. In Brooklyn I'd never met any boy who knew about existentialism or Simone de Beauvoir and I must have thought I never would again so I'd better seize the opportunity. And I would like to know what were your reasons. If you still remember.

THE GIRDLE

It's like your whole life, she said,
you're wearing a girdle,
then comes this one person . . .
With him you can take off the girdle
you didn't even know you had on.
The way the flesh spills, the ease,
you never dreamed . . . You get used to that
broad breathing, looseness of small daily things.
Then it happens. He's gone. Right away
the girdle is back on and this time
you know it.

CEMENT BACKYARD

My father had our yard cemented over.
He couldn't tell a flower from a weed.
The neighbors let their backyards run to clover
and some grew dappled gardens from a seed,

but he preferred cement to rampant green.
Lushness reeked of anarchy's profusion.
Better to tamp the wildness down, unseen,
than tolerate its careless brash intrusion.

The grass interred, he felt well satisfied:
his first house, and he took an owner's pride,
surveying the uniform, cemented yard.
Just so, he labored to cement his heart.

Remember the incredible shrinking man in the movie,
how small and smaller, scarily wee
he grows until his wife can cradle him
in a cupped palm, and smaller still,
till, with his tie askew and little shoes
untied he marches down the garden path,
into the tall grass, receding,
receding,
smaller and smaller he'll get and yet . . .
never quite gone, after all? After small,

there's always smaller, Zeno's arrow forecasting
the differential calculus. I always loved
that arrow, never arriving, like the little man,
never quite gone, mingling
with microbes, living his microscopic life.

I've sat for hours watching ice melt,
craggy peaks shifting shape on the sill,
tiny Rockies bored by the sun's death rays.
It takes time and more time till the last
chip becomes a drop, a stain,
yet not quite gone.

Or think of soap shrinking in the hand.
I chase it round the tub, capture the slippery
sliver, cup it in my palm till it's a glint.
I like to coax the last drops out of bottles,
hover over puddles narrowing from the outside
in, till there's just the dark blotch.

I have childhood friends who may be dead
except in memory, slivers sliding off
in the tall grass. Here I go too,
thinning, wisping, liquefying,
evaporating, but never quite
gone, not yet.

I dreamed I was in the afterlife, it was so crowded,
hordes of people, everyone seeking someone, staggering
every which way.

Who should I search for? The answer came quick: my mother.
I elbowed my way through strangers till I found her, worn,
like the day she died.

Mother, I cried, and threw my arms around her, but she
wasn't happy to see me. Her arms hung limp. Help me,
I said. You're my mother!

There are no mothers here, she said, just separate souls.
Everyone looks for their mother. I searched for mine, and found her
searching for her mother,

and so on, through the generations. Mothers, she said,
fathers, families, lovers are for the place you came from.
Here we're on our own.

Here is no help, no love, only the looking. This
is what death means, my child, this is how we pass
eternity, looking

for the love we no longer know how to give. I shuddered
myself awake. And yet—my child, she said, my child.
Or did I only dream
that word, dream within a dream?

Invite them all, the corner hot-dog man,
cops on the beat, butcher, baker,
street guys with their hands outstretched,
give everyone the best seat in the house,
front tables near the dance floor,
and the menu—forty courses, soup to nuts,
blood-red roasts, cake a creamy skyscraper,
booze gushing from vats, and topless waitresses,
bottomless too, why not?

Let the honeymoon begin right on the spot,
the groom fucking the bride in full
view, and while he's at it let him do
the bridesmaids too.
The bride should get the best man, it's her day.
And let the crowd join in, a free-for-all,
while the twenty-piece band plays
to beat the band, and while they're at it
why not beat the band, don't they deserve it?
And every goddamn minute videotaped
for *How to Plan Your Wedding Magazine*—
let them see
how truly lavish lavish weddings ought to be.

CHEWING THREAD

Chew a bit of thread, my mother said,
when you sew on a garment you're wearing.
If you don't chew when you sew on yourself,
your brain will get stitched up and stupid.
Wash the strainer right after you use it,
before the starch hardens. Check the stove
on leaving the house. Never forget
a thank you note. Double knot
the laces on your sneakers or you'll trip.
Never sit on boys' laps, don't ask why.
Take small bites when you eat,
especially with meat,
or you'll surely choke like your Uncle Albert,
may he rest in peace.

So to this day I chew, I do
as my mother told me. And I wonder
how it might have gone for Eve had she,
instead of a commanding single father,
possessed a mother such as mine to warn her:
Do not eat of the fruit of that tree, for he
who commands you is vindictive, unforgiving.
What he says, he means. Our future rests
in your hand now reaching towards the branch.
Draw back, shut your ears, step on the serpent
with your bare foot though it bite you.
When next you see Adam, say nothing.
His ignorance will be your bliss. Stay
in the walled garden. Dull it may be, but safe, safe.
Do not pluck that fruit, nor bite, nor chew.

Suppose I hadn't stumbled
over "dirigible" and had won the spelling bee,
and suppose I hadn't caught the chicken pox
the day of the baton twirlers' tryouts
and lay in bed reading *Gone with the Wind,*
my gleaming baton idle on the pillow,
and if not for my uncle's funeral
I'd have auditioned and been Ophelia,

driven mad with longing and frustration.
Suppose instead of a demure good night,
I'd murmured to the man who walked me home,
Why not come in for a drink?
And if only I hadn't mailed that bilious letter,
and all those times I spoke too hastily,
what if I'd held my tongue, and when
I kept a diffident silence, had spoken?

Suppose, that morning, I hadn't picked up the phone.
What was that click? his wife said.
Would everything have turned out differently?
Ah, the mistakes, the remorse, the sore,
raw delectations of regret,
the glorious life I might have led,
the succulent successes, the bold
triumphal poems I might have written.

THANK YOU NOTE

Thank you so much for the gift
of the green turtleneck sweater.
How thoughtful. But as it happens, green
is a color I never wear—
it doesn't suit my fair complexion—
and turtlenecks make me feel I'm choking.
Wool is itchy against my skin, also
it is too small, it tugs around the armpits,
and for all these reasons
which do not augur well,
I'm afraid I cannot marry you.

CONSIDER PAIN

Whether to greet it, treat it, as foe
or friend, reliable and steadfast?
Foe, the tempting choice,
means warfare, wreckage,
the blasted terrain, seizure in the night,
a poison of ill will flooding the veins.

Friend might be more canny.
Permit a short-term stay, get acquainted
with its habits, humors.
Still, offering pain too wide a berth
could be perverse, inviting
a clinging friend who overstays his welcome.

So maybe foe's the braver course,
an all-out battle, with a battle's risk.
Pain might become an occupying force
imposing its restrictions, seeking to snap
the frayed will, destroying
infrastructure, customs of a lifetime.

Then reconsider friend. Feigning friendship,
you may fool a pain into submission.

No, fuck all subtle strategies.
Pain is your foe. Defy. Fight back.

Friend, foe, foe, friend? All the while I waver
it works its way, burrowing,
unweaving the delicate webs . . .

A MOMENT'S PEACE

Peace, they say, is more
than mere absence of war.
The peace I seek is not world,
but private, the soul curled
on itself, sublimely still,
no noise or need or will.

Peace, elusive, awaited,
a longing unabated
until, while reading at night—relief
from a day's small wars and grief—

comes a quiet, emanating
from my book, penetrating,
embracing: the stillness I sought
by words and darkness wrought.
Peace—not to wonder at or grasp,
but savor its brief grand clasp.

WIND DUMMY

Scarecrow in uniform, the soldiers' toy,
a stuffed and patched-up boy.
They toss him here and there in roughhouse play,
and promise him an airplane ride—
a grown-up bombing mission.
His smooth, unfeatured face can't show his joy,
his keen anticipation or his pride.

Comes the ascent, and all is in position:
they grab him by the neck and hurl him out—
all mute and blank dismay—
to ascertain which way the wind is blowing,
in order to predict without a doubt
the place their bombs are going.

A sorry fate for any boy,
yet better than a human sacrifice,
an outworn vice.

Supposing we
are merely a sophisticated brand
of wind dummy,
dispatched by a more clever species' hands
to see which way the wind blows here below
in case they care to sample our condition.
How long before they come to a decision
is anybody's guess.
Till then we're at the mercy of the air,
hurtled by currents, landing who knows when
or where.

WINTER SOLDIER

2008

"They take all the humanness out of you"
said an ex-marine in the film of the Vietnam
veterans gathered in 1971 to describe
the sadistic acts they witnessed and committed
against the Vietnamese known to them as gooks
during their service in what they were trained to think
was their country's best interests such as searing
flesh raping and disemboweling all vividly
and in choked voices recounted

go see and hear for yourself and note when you do
the inventive male hair patterns sideburns bangs
whiskers beards goatees ponytails and other ingenious
designs using what you can grow yourself
flourishing on the heads of these tormented
men one of whom said it was terrible to watch
himself becoming an animal among animals.

If you are old enough
the hair will instantly recall what it was like then
the immense earnestness the courage to speak
out publicly to be unsophisticated
to show the self defenseless
all that is now considered foolish and uncool
and we'd best put behind us
but must we?

Yes there was awkwardness especially between black
and white witness the vociferous black man
in dark glasses demanding
why no one mentioned racism
when they talked about gooks it was pure racism

he said so why did no one say so
the white soldiers stood silent and nodded shamed
it was like that a lot back then everyone clumsy
fumbling trying to get near one another do something
useful with the bitterness and guilt not knowing how or what
everyone deferring maybe too humbly
to the loudest voices but they did speak truth and
were heard and something was achieved
some effort some germinating sense
of goodwill
not like now.

And while you sit watching in the dark ask yourself
why if this film came out in 1972
you are not seeing it until today and why
if these ex-soldiers found the moral wherewithal
to tell in public their cruel and ignorant deeds
in order to repent and exorcise them and as one said
so that others would not commit similar cruelties
and why too if this heartfelt testimony was
believe it or not read into the Congressional Record
is it happening all over again and will we
decades from now be watching another long
delayed film of men shattered by training in which
they chanted Kill Kill
Pray for War as a barracks lullaby.

Probably no there will be no movie of this war
because such sincerity never mind hair
is mocked these days and cruelty and torture
need not be hidden but are accepted as deeds
we must do for our country
our country
what is this country anyway
that we allow ourselves to become animals for?

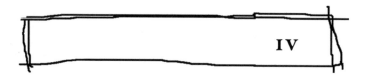

IV

Bucharest, Budapest, Berne . . . An uncanny,
unremarked coincidence, so many
notable cities starting with bumbling B.
Buenos Aires, Beijing . . . No letter comes close
excepting possibly P (Prague, Paris)
or M (Moscow, Madrid, Milan).

This I know because it's what I do
at night, till light, pursuing sleep. It keeps
at bay . . . Berlin, Barcelona, Bonn . . . the friends
sickening, dying . . . Belfast, Birmingham . . .
the work failing, the wars, the world fucked up . . .
Basel, Brussels, Baltimore . . . the best minds fled
to the electronic wasteland . . . Bruges, Boston . . .
A long list, long night. Bangkok, Basra, Baghdad . . .

These days it's a perpetual party
at the twilit moment when the guests
start leaving, first
the few acquaintances, protesting
how they'd love to stay, so sorry, thanks.
The room is thinned but still the party sparkles,
till a loved one makes excuses, then
another and another, grabbing their coats,
an epidemic of farewells, an avalanche
of leavetaking, though it's been a splendid party,
lots of food and drink, music, good vibes.
They murmur their good-byes, it's been . . . love you . . .
and you're left alone
with leftovers, crumbs of cheese, sour wine,
crumpled napkins, rancid butts, the chill
shudder as you sense it's time,
no one to talk to, nothing much to stay for.
You grab your coat,
leave the mess for the kids to clean up,
lock the door, tuck the key
under the mat, you're out of here.

HURRICANES

It was Henri Cole the poet
who uttered casually, as though they were nothing
much, the words "little hurricanes
of the heart"
during his talk on the sonnet,
its intricacies and near-infinite
adaptability to matters great
and small, particularly the above-
mentioned natural occurrences,
showing himself a generous soul
with images to spare, scattering
or rather sprinkling them among his hearers,
so that I can write a poem using
his words, little hurricanes of the heart,
for love of the words themselves,
and hurricanes, and sonnets that describe,
record, embody, or illumine them.
On the instant I heard Henri's phrase
in fact I felt a little liquid rush,
a small arterial tempest in the chest,
some happy coronary stir and squish
from dormancy, hardly a hurricane,
more like what they call a scattered shower.

As it happens I am writing this
during a rainfall, far from a hurricane,
just as this is far from a sonnet, merely
my *merci*
to Henri
for showering reviving
rain on dry hearts in dry spells.

IN BETWEEN

In between is richest, the fallings,
dusk, no word for the color of the sky,
the sodden air
dragging down day from light to blue,
from motion to indifference, or to rue.

Or like the slippery verge of love,
the succulent stage
before love asks for speech,
no word for that sweet leap
into need, or frenzy.

Drowning, they say, your past compresses,
passions and cravings compact into one
dense ball, ineffable, a lifetime sucked
into the in-between, the last fall
from feeling into the embrace
of cloud.

ON MY KNEES

What you been up to? my crabby neighbor asks,
idling, ogling, fat and lazy in the blessed shade.
Down on your knees, looks like. Don't tell me praying.

Maybe it's the scorching summer sun,
or the sting of my blotched, stone-scarred knees,
that makes me want to hurl a curt retort.

So many things can bring us to our knees.
Mopping the floor. A bout of love. Groping
for a contact lens, or keeping baby happy,

learning the art of the crawl,
or crouched in a corner, hiding from a blow,
hoping to escape on all fours.

Not praying, I told him. Gardening. But digging
down or upward is the same, I want to say.
Clawing and pawing in a sweat of toil,

asking the soil to yield us what we need,
taking a beating from the summer's blaze,
our facile fingers damp, hot, greedy,

and all the while entreating: Earth,
bear with my hands that strafe your skin.
Submit to fingering probes. We both know

how our affair will end. You'll open wide for me
and hungrily, claiming much more than hands.
You'll want me whole.

ECSTASY

Ecstasy, initially,
did not agree with me. A stupefying pill—
I'll sleep it off, I moaned. But you said walk,
walk the stupor and the faintness
off, wrapped me in a windbreaker
to walk into the wind on the hills
of Bolinas, below us the roiling ocean,
above, the wind slashing our faces.
My blood surged up again, its pressure rising
in ecstasy.

After the low, the high. We talked and laughed
all afternoon, afloat in a lukewarm tub,
face to face, running the water through
our lives, rinsing out our lives,
wringing out the past, then built a fire
and sat by the fire with food till late.

We passed our trip among the elements,
air, water, fire.
Now you are California earth, far from your place
of birth, Sarajevo, where the Germans came
in the front door and your family ran out the back.
Your first year in California you were crowned
prom queen for your beauty, fifty years later
gnawed from within. They found you with ants
crawling towards you, drawn by the smell. And I,
after that wind-whipped day, renounced
Ecstasy,
out of timidity,
because it is risky and unlawful,
and shouldn't the death of a friend like you
be equally unlawful?

TO THE YOUNGER LOVER

When you leave me, tell me
it's the tantrums you can't bear,
tell me I'm moody, flighty, unforgiving, given
to rash decisions followed by remorse,
say I'm cynical, selfish, hyper-
critical, spend too much time at the mirror,
on the phone, remind me
of the times I've kept you waiting . . .
Such a wealth to choose from,
tell me anything

except that it's the line of my jaw
when I lean to kiss your lips in the half-light,
the quavering, prophetic
sag, the line, no longer taut,
that marks the limit of your tolerance.

Time for lights out, the close of music class,
the room is dimmed, we're shoeless, the two-
and three-year-olds flopped down, sprawled on laps,
or curled alone, so many arms, legs,
awry like branches of a spreading tree,
a tree with years of growth to come, and my
resplendent child, flat on her back on the rug,
knees up, pressing into my side, we're hip
to hip, the teacher strums a guitar, singing
a lullaby I alone remember from far back,
I the sole grandmother among the long-legged
mothers, weary nannies, I try to sing
but find my throat is choked, surprise tears,
the warmth at my hip, the child's long lashes,
her perfection, the gladness like a geyser
shooting skyward, who ever thought
I'd know this moment, awe so keen it mimics
pain, what a relief to have the lights
restored, the music stop, the kids spring up,
the coats, hats, shoes, clutter, clatter
of departure, my heart slowed down.
I could die right now and wouldn't mind,
knowing the feel of her, the trust. We are
each other's for however long, warm hip to hip.

THE KEY

After the storm, on the beach, in front of the wrecked
house, its contents strewn on the sand, we found the key.

We held it, muddy, in our palms, we shivered
like children abandoned, then set it back on the sand.

The great key to the universe, we called it,
and left it for the sea with the rest of the rubble.

CHRISTMAS CACTUS

It thrives on darkness and the year's old age.
In spring it squats upon the sill,
a sullen plant of stubborn rage,
with spiky leaves that lack all force of will.

The solstice nears, and in its showers of light,
floods of color flourish, gaudy, loud,
all living things obediently bright:
the cactus' grim refusal is a shroud.

December's shadows spread like mud.
The cactus gulps the gloom, it eats the night,
erupts in rushed profusion, flowers like blood.
It teaches me to feed on dark's delight.

Then like a Christmas cactus shall I flare:
last-minute blood-red blooms against despair.

V

To liven things up at the sleep clinic—for as you can imagine, watching the insomniacs sleep and keeping track of the charts and flickering dials can be a soporific job—we decided to try something new. We invited our clients in pairs. Bring a friend, we advertised. Or sleep with a stranger if you must: leave it to us and we'll make all the necessary arrangements. There was no question of sex. They come to the clinic to learn to sleep; the other they can do well enough on their own, or at least it's not our concern.

It was amazing, what we saw. The longtime couples would execute an intricate ballet, limbs flinging and folding over each other, seeking, withdrawing, turning in tandem, searching for the other's skin even in sleep, one drawing a leg gently down the length of the other's leg or sending an arm through the air to land, after a sweetly arching drift, on a hip or shoulder, fingers stretching to touch then grasping or curling in happy relief. After a while they'd settle down, but never for more than a half hour or so, and then the dance would begin again, as if they were moving to music, each hearing the same silent music, each responding to the alternating legatos and staccatos in unison.

With the strangers, we tried at first to match them by the obvious criteria, age, type, body size, but this began to feel too much like a dating service—hardly our purpose—so we gave up and began matching them at random, first come, first served, so to speak. After all, they were asleep; it wasn't as if they needed to flirt or get to know each other or discover some interest they had in common. For their part, the clients so craved their sleep that they would do anything, lie down next to anyone, so long as it promised a good night's rest.

As you might expect, the strangers, asleep, moved more tentatively, but as the night wore on—and this didn't take very long, a couple of hours more or less—they grew more confident, tracing the outlines of the foreign body, coming to know it in the deepest of sleeps. Their dance had a more exploratory quality, compared to the longtime pairs; they weren't as finely attuned, but to compensate, there was the excitement of the unexpected, of discovery; their bodies appeared dynamic, in suspense, never quite knowing what they would find, whether they would find what they sought, or even what they were seeking. They suggested blindfolded dancers, although in a sense they were all blindfolded, intimates and strangers alike, since their eyes were closed.

You might have thought the sleepers would wake exhausted from such athletic repose, but in the morning they were refreshed, delighted, grateful for the rest they'd been missing at home. Impatient to start the day, they hastily helped us remove the paraphernalia, the electrodes and so on; we could barely keep them long enough to fill out the necessary reports. And they couldn't wait to return at night: some of them wanted to sleep with the same partner again, convinced that this particular pairing was responsible for their sound sleep, while others, just as in life, were driven by the spirit of adventure and change, eager for new partners no matter how satisfying their sleep had been.

The arrangements became so complicated that finally we had to devise a system of sleeping cards, like old-fashioned dance cards at a ball, so that people might sign up for new partners or the same ones, depending on their tastes and on how satisfying their sleep had been. Very soon our clinic became a popular nightspot, even more sought after than the neighboring clubs and bars—where in fact some of our clients spent the earlier part of the evening. But the sleep clinic was the culmination of their night out: evidently whatever our sleepers felt and did in their sleep was lodged someplace deeper in their consciousness, or unconsciousness, than their earlier, wide-awake dancing and drinking and flirting. Whatever they felt or did or learned about themselves and their partners, unawares, gave them some profound sense of contentment. And whatever they came to feel for the body dancing beside them in sleep could repose in the inaccessible depths, with none of the entanglements consciousness brings.

This rare simplicity we found intriguing, and difficult to account for. Some of us wanted to do a study of the elusive phenomenon, this sleep dancing-induced contentment, while others, more frivolously perhaps, wanted to undertake a survey inquiring whether any lasting relationships had evolved from our pairings at the clinic. But funds here, as for most scientific studies, are always tight. Our director, though he had indulged and, when he noted its success, eventually encouraged our Sleeping Together project, said no, such inquiries were beyond our scope. As long as our clients were sleeping longer and more soundly, he said, as long as the sleep clinic was thriving, we must be satisfied. To overstep the boundaries of our mission might dilute it and—a worst-case scenario—even tarnish our reputation.

The doctors, our families, everyone assumed we would choose the surgery right away. We were told it was easier and less problematic in infancy than later on. But we couldn't bring ourselves to expose a newborn to that kind of risk, plus God knows what pain and trauma. Was it really worth it simply to remove something that was even—it sounds crazy, I know, but—kind of cute? At least for the moment. We could always opt for the surgery later, when he was still small. And otherwise he was perfect, a beautiful boy. Maybe with a girl we might have felt differently. Everyone knows the whole beauty and conformity issue is tougher on girls, unfair as that is. But a boy . . .

Granted, it was a shock when we first saw it, right after he was born, when we were so glad it was all over and had been a normal birth. First the doctor's face showed genuine pleasure—relief, too—and then her expression changed, and the nurses' faces changed too: a stunned look, then a kind of horror, and then an unnerving silence fell over the room. They tried to wrap him up quickly but we knew something was amiss and insisted that they show us. We gasped—I remember I closed my eyes in disbelief. Of all the things we'd worried about, that all prospective parents worry about, who would ever have thought of this? We were holding hands; we squeezed them tight but didn't look at each other. Then immediately—he wasn't two minutes old—the doctor started talking about cutting it off. Not a word about the rest of him, how perfect everything else was.

We didn't fall in line as they expected. It wouldn't matter much until he started school, we figured, and then if it really bothered him it could probably be hidden. A lot would depend on how we handled it, and there was plenty of time to work that out. Our parents said we'd never be able to find babysitters once they saw; it was just too weird, it even gave them the creeps. That was plain to see, from the way they were reluctant to hold him, the way their lips curled ever so slightly and their fingers shrank back from the bundle in the blanket. That hurt us. Well, we told them, we'll have to find unprejudiced, broad-minded people. At some point in history we probably all had an appendage, so this was a reminder of what we came from. It didn't make him an animal, after all; he was a perfect little person, except for this throwback. And it could have been worse. He could have had a dread disease or some mental impairment. Would they prefer that?

We were reminded by the doctors that it wouldn't always stay so tiny. It would grow along with him. Think of him becoming a school-age kid, then an adolescent, they said. Think about him trying to play sports—it wouldn't be easy to hide in a football uniform, or tennis shorts, or in a locker room. And what about when he started going with girls? It was unfair, even cruel, not to remove it.

He could find ways of tucking it in, we said. It might even generate a certain cachet, depending on what kind of kid he turned out to be. If he was confident and felt good about himself—and we certainly intended to bring him up in that spirit—he could deal with it, maybe turn it into an asset. As far as girls and women, well, without going into gross detail, there might be a piquant appeal. That is, certain kinds of titillations he could offer that others couldn't. But naturally we didn't like to think about that sort of thing while he was just a tiny infant.

Besides, he couldn't be the only one. If there was something misprogrammed or awry in our genes—in the genes of one of us—surely there were others like us? Like him? There had been a few rare cases, the doctors said, but the parents always chose surgery promptly, before they took the child home from the hospital. And so they, the doctors, couldn't fathom our reluctance. Well, how about in other countries, we asked, say, third-world countries where they didn't have access to high-tech surgical procedures? They'd live with it, wouldn't they? They'd take what they'd been given and love it just the same. Maybe it was a test of what you could love. Parents loved babies with far worse deformities, if this should even be called a deformity.

Yes, somewhere in the world there must be others like him. We might find them. You can find anything online. Maybe they had some kind of group, some secret chat room where they exchanged advice about how they coped—though what a pity that they had to be so secretive. We could try to be more open, educate people about accepting differences. Why was it any different from a shrunken arm, like those thalidomide babies of the sixties, or a crossed eye, or a clubfoot? Nobody would choose those aberrations, of course, but there wasn't any dreadful social prejudice attached to them. Nobody thought of those people as less than human— as animals, almost. No one feared them or shunned them.

Of course we understood it was the suggestion of the primitive: something that wasn't supposed to be there, something we were supposed to have outgrown millennia ago. Well, apparently we hadn't outgrown it completely. It still lurked, in some of us.

So we took our baby home and we love him just as he is. There's no way of forgetting it; we see it all the time, changing him, bathing him. It curls up inside the diaper and no one who visits knows it's there. Everyone *oohs* and *aahs* as people do over newborns, and we think maybe we should start letting them know, acting as though it's nothing special, but we don't feel quite ready to do that. We do wonder all the time about how it could have happened, what was curled up unseen inside us—one of us. We talk about it, hesitantly; we're glad it can't be traced to either one of us and start us blaming, because there's never been anything like this in either of our families—as far as we know, that is. We agree that these things are random and inexplicable.

We wonder what else there may be about him that's different. I mean things we can't see as plainly as we see this, intangible things that may show up later on. But we don't talk about that. We wonder silently, and we wait.

I used to get a flush of sentiment, glancing at my parents in this ritualized pose, but now the more I study the photo, the more opaque, the more distant they become. My father is not even really offering himself to the camera. His self-satisfied smile—I'm pretty sure that's a smile and not clamped-teeth submission—is quite private, maybe a smile of complacency at possessing the satin-swathed woman in his arms, maybe a wisp of amusement long since gone to nothingness like the smoke of the cigar between his fingers that makes it impossible for my mother to clasp his hand, though I wouldn't rush to assign this any symbolic meaning. She has to rest her fingers against his open palm, leaving him free to hold the moss-green cigar which, dead as it appears, would have had a sharp, rank smell, like burning metal. In contrast to his opacity, his refusal to be caught out, my mother's smile is public, generic: she's pleased to be dancing in his arms, to have her pleasure witnessed and recorded. The harsh light smacking against her dress makes her body, pillowlike, seem encased in metal, the trailing ribbons standing out stiffly like an ornament on a 1950s car. Enough! I wish I hadn't looked so closely; I want to stop before I lose them entirely, before they become as remote and anonymous as the children in the background, whose patent leather shoes and white socks dangle above the floor, or the balding man on the right, whose raised hand hides his face in a gesture of . . . what? Horror, mortification, shock? Suddenly it's he who seems most authentic, who piques my curiosity. What has he glimpsed, outside the safety of the frame, that makes him hide his face?

The terrible mocking blue sky is finally gone and we are all glad, even the obedient ones who have taken up their daily rounds, pretending that life will be as before. The sky has paled, the warmth drained from the air, and still we come each morning with our boxes of chalk, our knee pads, our goggles. We need to be down here; it's where we belong, we're pulled to the barricaded streets. The foul air makes us cough but the searing in our throats spurs us on. The first morning after, only a few of us came, all with the same idea, to write in big letters on the streets. With every passing morning, those blazing azure mornings, others joined us. At first the police looked askance, then decided we were harmless. People stop to ask why we are down on our hands and knees, why months later we keep writing on the streets. Often they join us.

We write the same thing each day: I was in my car, on the bridge, I saw . . . On the bus, a woman on a cell phone started screaming . . . I was feeding the baby, I had the radio on . . . The phone rang, it was my sister-in-law, my girlfriend, my downstairs neighbor, my ex-husband . . . I was in the coffee shop, at the office, at the dentist, in class, from my hospital bed I saw it all out the window . . . I was in Honolulu, in London, in Paris, in Sydney . . .

The city sent people to question us. They were gentle, at least at first. Everyone was gentle, at first. We were breaking no laws. It is not yet against the law to write on the streets. It would be hard to arrest us anyway—we are too many. Now at night, to deter us, they hose the streets down. (It seems never to rain anymore, as if the sky holds back its tears.) See, they say, your writing is washed away. No matter. We'll write it again: The butcher's wife was in there. The girl in my yoga class was in there. The super's daughter. My daughter. My father. My wife.

A man from the city pleaded with us: Go back to your lives, he said. Or at least write something new.

We would like to write something new, we are very tired of our stories, but we don't know what the next sentence should be.

We have tried to proceed to the next sentence. But to write, you must know something, and we know nothing beyond the intolerable questions that assail us. Grief, at an infernal temperature, has burnt knowledge out of us. We try to write the next sentence, and senseless, contrary words come out, as if from a cauldron.

What is the just path? Revenge is tempting, but also loathsome and useless. Can we love our country if we cannot love the voices that claim to be our country? Could this have happened? Look, over there, it happened. Terrible things have always happened to people. Why not to us? But why should such things happen to anyone? Who did it? Who are "they"? Who is innocent? Who is guilty? How can we tell? Is it war again? Then win the war. But don't kill anyone. Be prudent. No, be bold. No, a show of strength will only make things worse. The voices that blame us stir our rage—this is no time for blaming. The voices that extol us stir our rage—this is no time for smugness. Will some voice, please, speak an intelligent word in public? We long to hear an intelligent word. No, we long for silence. Enough words have been spoken. The words are ashes poured into our ears. Deafened, we seek the right path. But with our eyes coated with ash, how can we see any path, or truth, or justice?

We cannot write such sentences, made of useless words that seethe in the head. Of that blue and fire morning, we can only write what we know for certain: I would have been in there except I slept late . . . I had a toothache . . . I got caught in traffic . . .

But our sisters . . . Our brothers . . .

This we imprint on the streets, as if the soft chalk might cut grooves in the pavement. We cling to our stories, we take root in our stories like the nymph who took root in a tree and became its prisoner. Unlike her, we will regain our shapes— almost. We will do what is needed; we will write the next sentence. Only not yet, not here on the bleak brink of November.

NOTES

"Saint Alexius's Mother": I found the story of Saint Alexius in a display at the Basilica of San Clemente in Rome. The poem follows the Greek legend, in which Saint Alexius lived in the first half of the fifth century.

"So You Want to Be a Druid": The Druid initiation rites are described in Robert Graves's book *Claudius the God.*

"TraumaMan": In 2005, National Public Radio ran a brief story about a torso doll called TraumaMan, used to train prospective surgeons in medical schools. At the time, the doll cost several thousand dollars and could be used repeatedly for six kinds of operations.

"Two from Catullus": Latin from *The Poems of Catullus,* trans. James Michie (London: Panther Books, 1972).

"Shrinking Verlaine": French from *One Hundred and One Poems by Paul Verlaine* (Chicago: University of Chicago Press, 1999).

"Not Quite Missed Connections, Craigslist.org": The online site Craigslist.org runs a page called "Missed Connections," on which people post messages seeking out appealing strangers glimpsed in public places.

"Wind Dummy": Again on National Public Radio, I heard former secretary of state Colin Powell describe the technique of throwing a dummy out of an airplane to test the prevailing winds, in preparation for bombings.

"Winter Soldier": In 1971 in Detroit, Vietnam Veterans Against the War sponsored a public inquiry into war crimes committed by American troops in Vietnam. The event was filmed and attended by press and TV correspondents but never received wide coverage. The film, which was shown in New York City in 2006, is rarely seen.